Paper Quilling Handbook

A Beginners Guide for Learning How to Handcraft Stylish Paper Quilling Pattern Designs With Quilling Instructions, Tools, Supplies, and Techniques to Get You Started

By

Zelda Cobb

Copyright © 2022 – Zelda Cobb

All rights reserved

No part of this publication may be reproduced, distributed, or transmitted in any form or by any means, including photocopying, recording, or other electronic or mechanical methods, without the prior written permission of the publisher, except in the case of brief quotations embodied in reviews and certain other non-commercial uses permitted by copyright law.

Disclaimer

This publication is designed to provide competent and reliable information regarding the subject matter covered. However, the views expressed in this publication are those of the author alone, and should not be taken as expert instruction or professional advice. The reader is responsible for his or her own actions.

The author hereby disclaims any responsibility or liability whatsoever that is incurred from the use or application of the contents of this publication by the purchaser or reader. The purchaser or reader is hereby responsible for his or her own actions.

Table of Contents

Introduction 6

Chapter 1 8

Paper Quilling Fundamentals 8

  What is Paper Quilling? 8

  The Evolution of Paper Quilling 9

  Pros and Cons of Paper Quilling 10

Chapter 2 16

Paper Quilling Tips and Techniques 16

Chapter 3 23

Getting Started With Paper Quilling 23

  Basic Tools and Supplies 23

    Precut Quilling Strips 23
    Slotted Tool 25
    Quilling Needle 25
    Glue and Adhesive 26
    Scissors 27
    Tweezers 28

    Ruler 28
    Straight Pins 29
    Quilling Template Board 29
  Advanced Quilling Tools 29

    Quilling Combs 30
    Quilling Molds 30
    Crimper 30
    Fringing Scissors 30
    Border Buddy 31
  Paper Quilling Basic Shapes 31

Chapter 4 55

Paper Quilling Pattern Designs 55

  Flower Pendant 55

  Flower Frame 66

  Snowflake 70

  Necklace and Earring 76

  Butterfly 83

  Birthday Cake 97

  Birthday Card 102

  Owl 108

Chapter 5 117

Fixing Paper Quilling Common Mistakes 117

Chapter 6 126

Paper Quilling FAQs 126

Conclusion 131

Introduction

There are thousands of artworks in the world today, but then, only a few of them have the versatility that we all love. Most of them suffer the effect of stereotypes, and the others require that you spend tons of money just to start up with the craft. However, there is a craft that fulfills all the good sides of the above parameters. It is versatile, cheap to start up, and cradled with a lot of fun, and this craft is called paper quilling.

Paper quilling is an art that involves rolling up strips of paper into different coils. You get to decorate cards, books, and several other items that formally were bare and severe. Paper quilling has been noted to bring life to the surroundings, events, and even to those with emotional issues, among many others. However, as simple as this art seems, it still requires that you pay attention to very intricate details that others are very likely to ignore. For example, you'd be working with a lot of glue. You want to know how much glue you should dot on a surface, how much you should scrape off, where and how to apply the glue and all those other details that'd push you to be a professional in this craft.

You also want to know how you can coil out different shapes from paper. Did you know that it is possible to craft out a teardrop from paper? Did you also know that you can craft out the loveliest butterfly from colored quilling strips of paper? There are tons of things you can do with this craft, and it helps even more that you don't have to do it alone.

On a cool day, you and your family could stay up all night and build up a paper castle. This book, *Paper Quilling Handbook*, will guide you through all you need to know to master the art of making eye-catchy paper quilling designs.

Stay hooked!

Chapter 1

Paper Quilling Fundamentals

Paper is obtained from various fibrous materials like wood pulp. Its value is almost very minimal, but then, the purpose for which it can be used cannot be underestimated. One very aspect in which paper is heavily used is in arts and crafts. Arts and crafts is a broad topic, and it utilizes anything—scraps, high-quality materials, anything. Paper is one of those things, and here, we would focus intently on Paper Quilling.

What is Paper Quilling?

The term 'Paper Quilling' dwells around using rolled paper strips to make the most intricate and ornate designs. These rolled strips usually adhere to surfaces like wooden plaques in three-dimensional patterns and coordinate arrangements. You get to embellish pots, mundane boxes and surfaces, plain walls, and even make jewelry with this art.

To start quilling paper, you'd only need a couple of kick-off materials. You wouldn't even need to sit by some table and then cut out strips of paper of all sizes.

In art and craft stores, you'd find pre cut–out strips which can take the form of different patterns, colors, and shapes. Some folks like myself, who have sheets of paper lying around, with absolutely no use at all, could decide to cut them up into nice sizes, though. The choice is left to you.

Then, next is the quilling tool which works a lot of magic! You can get your extremely flattened paper strips into nicely rolled pieces with it. You would want to imagine the supercoiled shell of a snail right now for visualization. Yes! You could create the most ornate and whorled flowers with these coiled pieces and even get your home embellished. The quilling tool, however, doesn't just make coils. It makes all shapes come nicely out of paper.

The Evolution of Paper Quilling

Origin of Paper Quilling

Paper quilling dates back to the Renaissance when it was employed to adorn books and religious artifacts such as crosses by Italian and French nuns. These paper quilling pioneers would utilize paper strips clipped from gilded book's edges to create quilled artwork.

By the 18th century, the trade had spread throughout Europe and was particularly popular among women regarded as "ladies of leisure." Quilling became popular in the U.S. as the country became colonized but went out of fashion in favor of other hobbies like sewing, sketching, and jewelry design.

Paper Quilling In Recent Times

Paper quilling has made a comeback because of social media's emergence and the capacity to connect and explore new art forms. It's simple to get started because many crafters already have the majority of the necessary supplies. Cards, jewelry boxes and invitations can all be embellished with this hobby. The fact that this art is simple to grasp for both kids and adults contributes to its appeal. Paper quilling will be a lot of fun for you if you have a creative spirit, a whole lot of ingeniousness and a knack for eye-hand coordination.

Pros and Cons of Paper Quilling

Even though paper quilling is an interesting craft to indulge in, it wouldn't hurt to be educated on its advantages and disadvantages.

Pros

1. Quilling could be a great way to start a business. If you've always been fascinated in art and craft and want to commercialize your work, you can consider it. Quilling can be used to make jewelry, posters, greeting cards, portraits, purses, boxes and even dreamcatchers. It's always wonderful to turn your interest into a full-fledged career.

2. Anyone, at any moment, can master this remarkable art form. Even if you are a novice, you need not be concerned because mastering this type of art does not necessitate being a genius or possessing a degree. It's simple and a lot of fun! If you want to pursue quilling professionally, you'll need to get familiar with all of the tools, and learning takes a lot of time and effort. However, quilling is a simple skill to master, aside from these minor concerns.

3. Quilling is a very cost-effective technique. Quilling requires only paper strips, glue, and a tool. If purchasing a quilling tool is out of the

question, a needle and push pins can be used. In reality, if you look about your home, you'll find a variety of quilling tools that you may use to create your own unique designs. You don't need a large canvas or an intricate painting set to accomplish quilling. It is exceedingly simple, cost-effective, and inexpensive.

4. Quilling is a really efficient stress reliever. It is, in fact, both meditative and therapeutic. You're rolling papers to make a variety of unique shapes. Finishing a quilling design takes a long time, but the technique might help you relieve stress. Quilling is similar to a finger and brain exercise. The more you can keep them busy, the happier you will be.

5. Quilling stimulates the brain and aids in the creation of wonderful designs. The rest is entirely up to your own imagination once you've mastered the fundamentals. You must be creative and innovative if you visualize a picture and try to recreate it using this art style. As a result, we can conclude that quilling is nearly like a

cognitive exercise, and if you practice quilling frequently, you will see a significant improvement.

6. It's usually a good idea to keep your children busy with important activities. A quilling kit is more absorbing and exciting than video games or cell phones. Quilling is a great way to keep a child occupied and attentive. When a child encounters this lovely type of art, he or she learns to be more calm and inventive. Quilling, a creative and aesthetic activity, has been shown to aid with cognitive growth in kids.

7. As previously stated, quilling stimulates your creativity. Because quilling can be used to make so many different items, your ideas and creativity can turn this part-time activity into a full-time business.

Cons

1. For beginners, some everyday items can be modified and used as quilling tools; however, this is not a long-term solution. If you

want to make quilling a career, you'll require advanced professional quilling tools, which might be costly and can be tough using them regularly.
2. One of the most significant drawbacks of quilling is how long it takes to produce a single design. If quilling is your pastime, it may interfere with your other interests because it becomes addictive after a while, but you can't really stop except you complete a design. Even for expert quilling artists, finishing a design on time might become increasingly challenging.
3. If you're proficient at quilling, you can certainly consider beginning a business, but you'll need to categorize the work well in order to make a profit and keep your business running smoothly. Quilling is not a very viable business option because time is a major factor.
4. If you're a perfectionist who wants to make a beautiful design, you'll need to use extreme caution when applying the proper amount of

glue. It can ruin your entire design if you don't use it correctly.
5. Quilling allows you to create a variety of unique items. Choosing the correct quilling tools for your work, on the other hand, might be a daunting task. Beginners are most times unable to appropriately select the right quilling tools.

Notwithstanding these little stumbling blocks, quilling is a profound art form that necessitates a great deal of patience, devotion, ingenuity, and creativity. It is highly relaxing as well as a fantastic exercise for all art enthusiasts. Many people have gone on to become renowned quilling artists and have been successful in their endeavors.

Chapter 2

Paper Quilling Tips and Techniques

Paper quilling is a lot of fun, but it might be difficult to learn if you are just starting out. Learning some important tips and techniques, on the other hand, can make all the difference – we've got you covered!

1. Use a variety of colorful backgrounds. A pure white background might be obtrusive and draw attention to every flaw, but a colored background is more forgiving and offers somewhat less contrast to your quilled shapes. It'll help people focus on precisely whatever you want them to — your design's overall beauty!

2. Ensure that each coil has a perfect center. A needle tool is not required to build beautiful coils. A slotted tool, when used correctly, can provide you with a round center without being crimped. After you've gotten to your strip's end, keep twisting your quilling tool until the tool gives way.

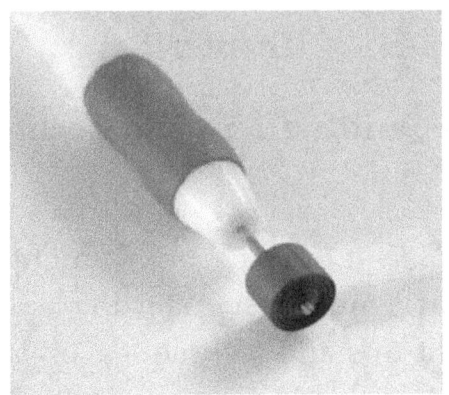

The tool rips the piece of paper that would have served as the crimp, resulting in a flawless coil. If your quilling tool isn't up to the challenge, smoothen out the crimp with a pin or piercing tool.

3. Tear rather than snip. Certainly, you want to keep your shapes as clean as possible and cover all seams.

However, there are situations when hiding is not an option. You can tear your quilling strip's end rather than use scissors to snip it if you don't prefer how the sharp paper seams look. The joint will be softer as a result of this.

4. Roll with the quilling strip's edge, not against it. When quilling paper is cut, the blade cuts it in a descending manner from above. This causes both long edges to roll down somewhat. The result is so subtle that it's difficult to notice with the human eye, but when you pass the strip through your fingers, you can feel it.

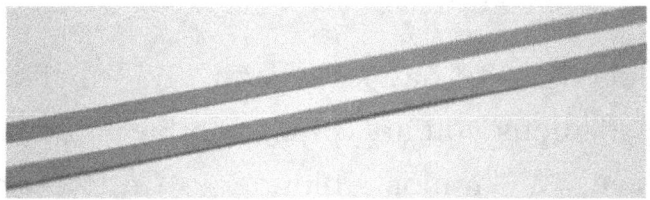

Roll with the curvature (the curve facing downward should face down) for a more precise coil. It may be difficult to achieve this on your first few attempts, but omitting this step will not affect the appearance of your quilling. However, once you pay close attention, you'll find that doing things this way becomes practically second nature.

5. For a grippy roll, double up your strips. When quilling an even more larger coil, the center will almost always break away from the quilling tool before you are finished. At that point, your only option is rolling the remainder by hand. However, you may avoid all of this by starting your coil by simply doubling the strip: this will retain things where it belongs. You can do this by folding over your first strip or layering two strips over each other.

6. Nobody is flawless, and no matter how meticulous you are, practically every project will have a minor blunder. Cuticle nippers usually come in handy in this situation.

Nippers, which can be found in the nail care section of any drugstore, will allow you to gently snip off an unequal edge or clear excess glue after it has dried.

7. A quiller's best buddy is a sponge, and a setup such as the one below is magical.

The damp sponge stops your glue from drying out and blocking the tip, while the container keeps the bottle of your needle-tip glue upside down, making it ready to use for subsequent times. The sponge's surface can also be used to wipe off any adhesive that clinged to your fingers. Simply split a kitchen sponge in half and place it inside a small bowl or dish to make your own. You may also build a setup that fits inside your quilling kit.

8. So you forgot to put your cap on, and the tip of your needle is now blocked even with the sponge technique discussed above that you probably did not follow through with. It's fine; there is still hope, however! You can unhook the tip with an eye pin and return to making your quilling craft.

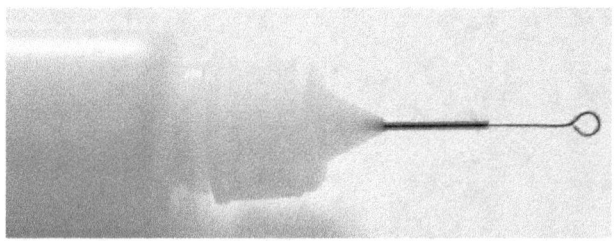

The blunt edge of an eye pin makes it a safer alternative to a sewing pin. Just don't leave the eye pin in the tip for too long, as it may rust and stain your glue.

Other tips you should take note of as a beginner include the following;

1. When you take a quilling stripe in your hand, you'll notice that one side of the strip has a smoother feel compared to the other. Keep the side with the smoother side feel as the outermost one when rolling the strip to make any form.
2. Purchase pre-made paper strips; creating paper strips yourself can be difficult for beginners.
3. Before beginning any project, learn the basic shapes and how to use the common quilling tools.
4. Apply glue with extreme caution; a smudge-free final piece is crucial for the desired aesthetic. It's also quite easy to make a mistake, so use a precision tip applicator and carefully apply the glue.

Chapter 3

Getting Started With Paper Quilling

Basic Tools and Supplies

Even when you have your paper ready before you, you still need to know what tools you'd need to cut them up into shapes and then coil them. Here are some of the tools you'd need; some are basic and others are additional tools you can get to make more professional-looking and advanced paper quilling designs.

Precut Quilling Strips

Like it was mentioned earlier, you could decide to go through the stress of having your paper cut up into different shapes or not. Now, this option here cancels out the stress of cutting paper strips, especially as a beginner, which may prove a little challenging when you start. It's advisable to purchase precut quilling strips, as a beginner. All you'd need to do is walk into where art and craft supplies are sold and then get your precut strips.

With these strips, you can proceed to craft out your quilling piece in no time. If you are also worried about getting the right color or shape, you can cast that aside. The precut quilling strips come in several colors and dimensions, leaving you to shop based on your preference. The following widths are the standard width dimensions that you'd find for the precut quilling strips;

- 1/16-inches
- ¼-inches
- 1/8-inches
- 3/8-inches

The most commonly used strip is the last one, 1/8-inches. Most crafters have found it highly easy to work with and coil up.

Slotted Tool

If you have ever wondered what tool was used to quill paper strips, here is your answer—the slotted tool. The tool has a slot in the central portion of its length that helps to keep your quilling paper held down firmly. That way, you'd have no hitch coiling the paper up.

The issue with this slotted tool is that it leaves folds at the middle of the coil where the needle stays. Usually, the folds are not too obvious, but if you do not want them to affect the look of your project, you could switch the slotted tool with a quilling needle.

Quilling Needle

The function this needle plays is quite similar to the one that the slotted tool plays. However, the method of operation contrasts sharply. There isn't a slot at the tip of a quilling needle. But unlike the slotted tool, it produces a tighter center with no hole in the middle.

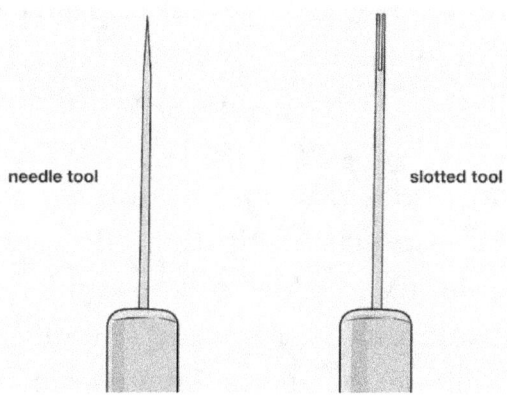

Here, you wound the strip of paper you want to work with around a needle, with one of your fingers exerting the right pressure to the wound paper. Even though this technique is quite tricky, it will help give you a nice and neat finish.

Glue and Adhesive

When you wound paper into a coil, you definitely would not expect the paper to just stay in place. This is where the glue comes in. The edges would need to be held down with glue as a concluding step. All you'd need to keep the end of the coil neatly sealed is a perfect swap of glue. Most times, water-based glue works perfectly for this purpose.

You might also want to consider using colorless and transparent glue. The glue usually doesn't leave marks once it dries. It just helps to hold the end of your coil in place, and that's mostly it. You also would need a bottle with a tip that is structured for precision – this is called the precision tool glue applicator, a small plastic container with a precision tip that allows applying just the proper quantity of glue to your quilled piece's end. This is an absolute must-have for any quiller. It assists you in consistently producing flawless quills.

If the glue bottle you have doesn't have the tip mentioned above, you could create one for it. You could replace the head with something that has a narrow mouth. That way, you would save yourself the trouble of dealing with a very messy project.

Scissors

Scissors are great cutting tools, but then, you want to make sure that it is shaped to aid your cutting. Scissors with pointed tips and light bodies usually work well for quilling and trimming your paper into the right dimensions.

Tweezers

Tweezers are used to get rid of dried glue from the surface of your project. They are also used to get rid of the flabby coils from your project's board so that you can maintain their shape. There are several tweezers available out there; one is the eyebrow tweezing tool. The tool could be difficult to handle when working with your project, but tweezers with long handles and forks would work best.

Ruler

With rulers, you can determine the dimension of the paper you'd need for a particular kind of coil. Rulers are also useful in ensuring that your project piece is centralized on the board on which the pieces are arranged. You could also find some rulers, which have their ends equipped with measuring aids and templates that aid in increasing the sizes of the coils.

Straight Pins

These pins work as temporary adhesives. You use them to secure one coil to the next while tracing out a pattern so that the coils are held together in one place.

Quilling Template Board

This board acts as a guide in helping you to determine the particular shape and size of quills that you'd need for your project. You won't want to miss out on not getting this tool if you are just started out.

Advanced Quilling Tools

Although the basic tools already discussed are a good place to start off, you will want to consider getting additional tools if you want to make more professional-looking and advanced paper quilling designs. These additional tools are given below;

Quilling Combs

These are similar to conventional combs; however, they have smaller metal prongs. You can achieve a similar result with your hair comb, but the comb's bigger teeth pose a challenge. Paper flowers and coils of the same type are made with a quilling comb.

Quilling Molds

These are plastic molds with various-sized domes. They create jewelry and other projects by forming a quilled paper dome.

Crimper

These are two protruding, revolving plastic pieces. When you roll the paper between the tool, it creates a crimped look.

Fringing Scissors

These are specialist scissors with several blades, usually 4-5 pairs. They're utilized to add a decorative touch to the edges of flowers.

Border Buddy

With the use of a pyramid-shaped tool with various levels and sizes, this is used to make hollow quilled shapes. Coil the paper strips all around the border buddy tool to make some fantastic hollow-shaped coils that can be used alone or in combination to make brilliant items.

Paper Quilling Basic Shapes

Paper quilling only begins to make a lot of sense when you delve into the topic of shapes. The area where you shape your paper strips is the part that takes the longest time to do. This area will also require you to exercise as much patience as possible. So, here, we will discuss the basic shapes that you can work with while quilling.

Also, you must have the basic tools and supplies previously discussed before you start making shapes.

Open (Loose) and Closed (Tight) Coils

The first thing you'd want to learn as a beginner is how to craft out circles from quilling paper. These circles usually serve as bases for the other shapes. To make these coils, we would go in steps;

1. Fix a quilling paper into the slot of the slotting tool. You could also work with a quilling needle if you wish.

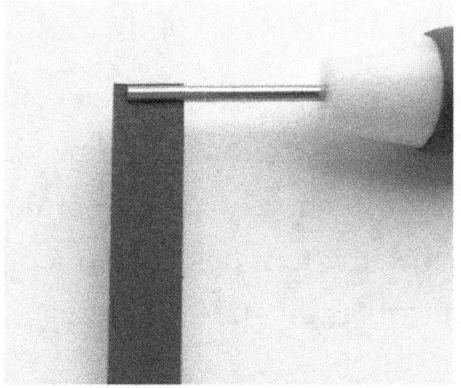

You should ensure that the ends of the paper and that of the slot match up with little to no error in alignment.

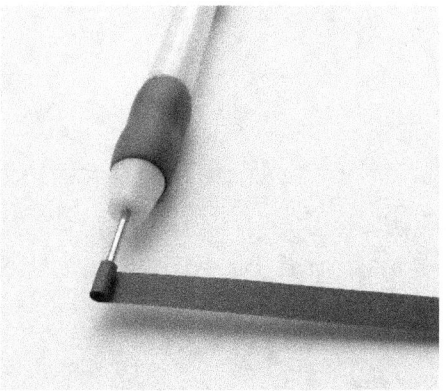

If you'd prefer that the coil has folds at the middle, you could work with the slotting tool. Usually, the coil is hardly visible, but if you want it to be very prominent, leave the paper suspended over the end of the slotting tool.

2. After fixing the paper, rotate the tool in a direction that faces you, or either way. It depends on which direction you find more comfortable. Ensure that the tool lies on a smooth platform as you rotate it, as illustrated below.

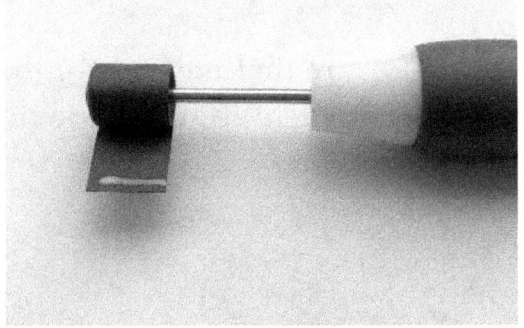

Make the other end of the uncoiled strip straight by pressing it down with the tip of your finger. The finger should be from the other hand that is not rotating the tool.

3. If you want to make a coil with a closed-end, you'd need to work with glue. As you approach the end of the paper strip, use the glue bottle with the specialized tip to apply a thin layer of glue to the end. Ensure that the coil doesn't increase in size or grow less tight as you get it out of the slotting tool. An example of a closed coil is illustrated below;

For an open coil, pull the tool out of the coil, while taking no care for the slight loosening of the coiled strips. Once the coil expands, apply a slight smear of glue to the end of the strip you wish to stop the coil. Then, press the coiled end to the glue to hold it down in place.

Teardrop and Its Variations

This shape will be built with the open coil as a base. So, to start with this, ensure that you must have completed the process of making the open coil described above.

1. Use the tip of your thumb and forefinger to grip the open coil. You want to ensure that the hand you are using to hold the open coil is the hand you won't be using to coil the paper strip.

2. With your hand, press down a side of the coil down at the point you want the tip of the tear to inclined towards.

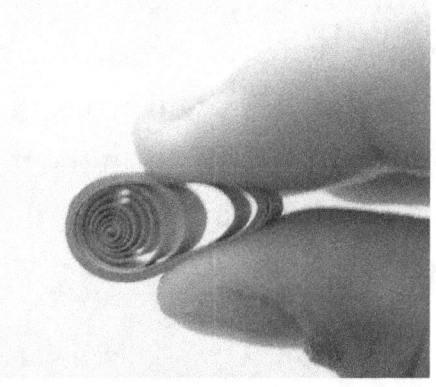

This technique will instantly give you a coil that is shaped in the form of a teardrop.

3. There are different ways by which you can alter the shapes of the teardrop. For example, by bending the arch that forms the teardrop with your thumb, you can work out a slight shape twist at the tip. That will work out without you having to destroy the coils in the middle. You can roll the teardrop around a quilling tool to improve the general outlook.

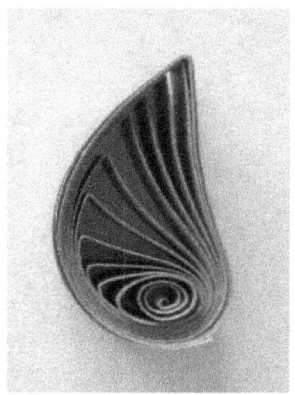

4. Another style is the one shown below. To achieve it, all you need to do is press the side arch of the coil around your quilling tool so that the curve comes out more visibly.

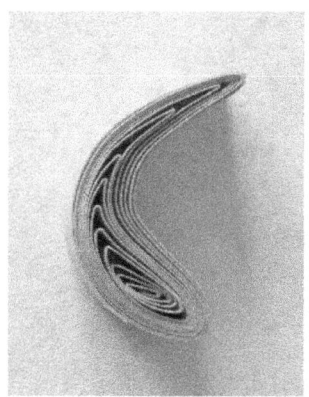

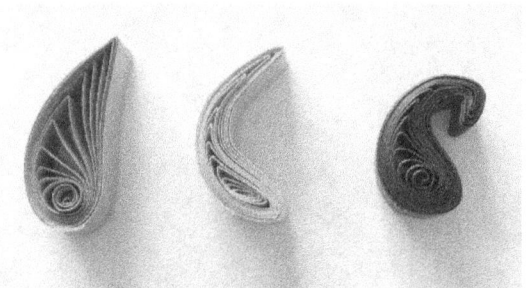

Marquise/Eye

A marquise is another shape built on the teardrop structure.

1. Once you have made the teardrop, pinch one of the ends of the teardrop.

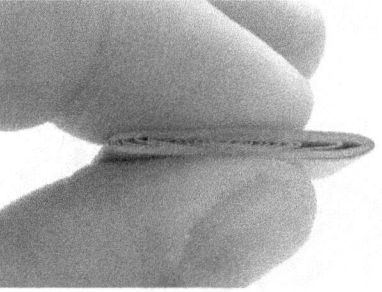

2. The final outline of the marquise depends on the number of coils you press down. It also depends on where you fix the coil's central point. To work out different structures and designs of coils, all

you need to do is apply more pressure to the center of the coils.

The illustrations below describe the other designs you could come out with at the end of this step.

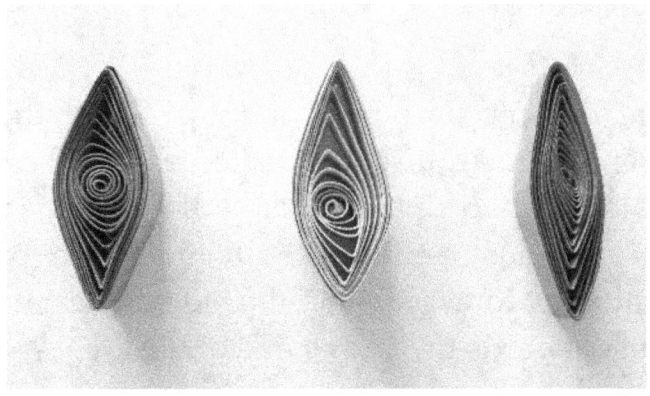

Tulip

This tulip is also developed from the marquise. All you need to do here is make the marquise shape. After that, move on to one of the edges of the coil. Pinch out a nub at the side arches with two of your fingers from the edge. The general outlook should look like the one illustrated below;

Slug

The slug doesn't start from a tulip, no. It, however, starts from the marquise we created earlier. To create a slug, hold the two tipped ends with your thumb and middle finger, just as illustrated below. Then, press the tip of your forefinger against the side arches at a point that is just towards the end of one of the arches.

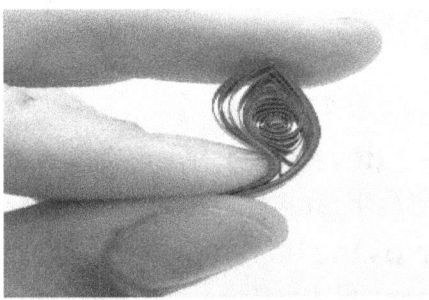

You could also use a quilling tool to create the 'slug' effect. However, you should ensure that whatever you do for one end is repeated for the other end. That way, you end up with the perfect 'slug' shape. Below is another illustration you could use as a guide.

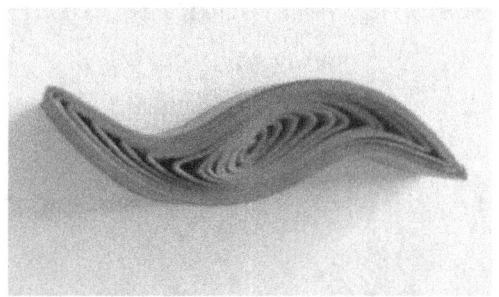

Diamond/ Square and its Variations

You'd also start from the marquise shape when creating a diamond or square shape with your paper strips. The moment you are done with the marquise, turn it around at an angle of 90-degrees. Then, pinch the two ends to form arrowed edges. Those arrowed edges alongside the major body will fetch you the shape of an actual diamond. The diamond illustration lies below;

To get a square, all you'd need to do is press the two arrowed edges towards each other. The illustration below describes what you should get finally.

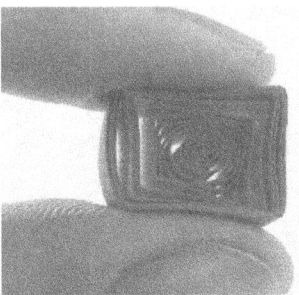

There are different ways you could design the square you finally get. These variances depend on the edges or corners you pinch with your fingers. We will be using the illustration below;

- The square at the left was obtained when enough pressure was applied to the outermost edges.

You'd also notice that the inner coils looked rounded.
- The one at the middle was obtained with the aid of an open coil. The open coil was pressed to one edge, and then, the corners at the opposite edges were pinched together.
- The last square was obtained by pressing the coils down on the two turns. This technique provided the special central coil design below.

Rectangle and Its variations

A rectangle is a form of a quadrilateral, and usually, the quadrilateral shapes are formed by inclining four edges to one another. Each edge should roughly form an angle of 90-degrees or more to the horizontal. Learning to construct quadrilaterals in paper quilling is very important when you need to fill empty angles.

Below are a couple of variations that can be accomplished via a rectangle.

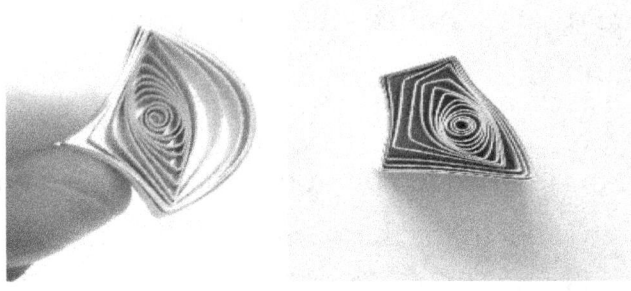

Semi-Circle

To create a coil that is shaped in the form of a semi-circle, you'd need to start from open coils. All you need to do is form two base angles by pressing them close to each other. Then, you leave the arch above the inner coils. You could also create a semi-circle by fixing one side of an open coil to a regular surface. Then, use the tips of your fingers to exact enough pressure downwards. Ensure that your fingers slide from one side to the other very neatly. Either method should get you something that looks like the one in the illustration below;

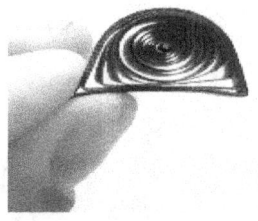

To get your semi-circle having the moon's outline, you could easily curve the straight end of the semi-circle in, i.e., the diameter. The illustration below describes what you should eventually get as a result.

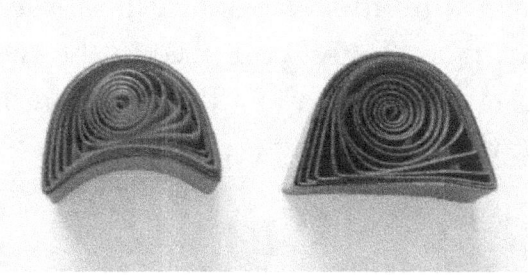

Triangle and Its variations

To craft a quilled triangle, all you need to do is to start with the teardrop pattern. From there, bend two more ends closely together with your fingers. You could also press one end against a regular surface with your fingers if you wish. What you get should look closely like the one shown below.

There are different triangle variations you can work with. You can build something that bears a close resemblance to the fins of a shark just by caving in the ends of your triangle. As you cave in the two ends, you could choose to have the third edge straight off. Below is an illustration of a triangle variation.

Arrow

To craft an arrow, you'd need to start with a teardrop.

All you need to do is push the middle of the coil's base inwards. You could use a quilling tool for that. As you push the middle of the base in, you'd want to ensure that you have the two edges pressed closely to each other.

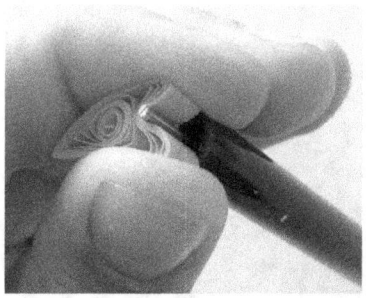

When you are done pressing the middle down, let go of the tool, and curve the sides up with your fingers. What you get finally should look closely like the illustration below.

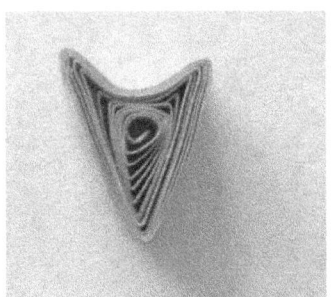

Arrowhead

To make an arrowhead, you would need to start with a teardrop. With the pointed end in hand, press down until you cannot go further. Then, allow your fingers to push their way downwards so that you create a side incline.

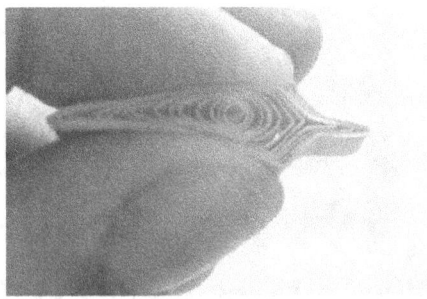

Heart

To craft a heart, you'd need to start with a teardrop. Push at the end of the shape with the pointed edge of your quilling tool. Just press the tip down through a distance that is enough to fetch you a slight dent.

After that, remove the tool from the tip and then gently cave in the sides of the coil to get the real 'heart' shape.

Pentagon and Star

Pentagons are made from semi-circles. To start, create a long semi-circle. Then, press the middle of the flattened edge down, like you would do when creating a tulip.

This edge will stand as the apex of the pentagon. The apex should be centralized, while the arch that lies downward should be squared up. What you get should look closely like the one illustrated below.

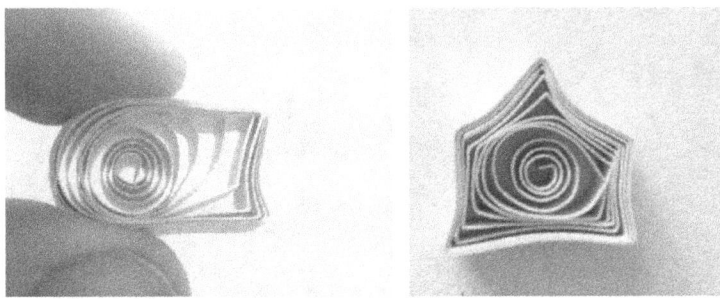

To create a star, all you need to do is apply enough pressure in five different arches, either with the aid of your fingers or your quilling tool. After that, you can then proceed to carve the ends into bright and sharp tips.

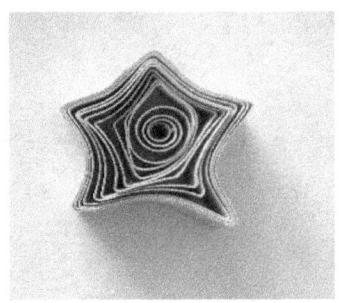

Holly Leaf

The holly leaf has been recorded as the most difficult shape to make. That is also why we are treating this shape as the last. If you are going to try this shape out as a beginner, you must be more than familiar with the rest of the shapes.

To craft this leaf, you'd need to begin with a marquise shape. First, you'd need to fix in a pair of tweezing tools within the coils of the marquise, like it was illustrated below. Ensure that the tip of your tweezing tool is only enclosed around 1/3-inches of your coil.

With your tweezing tool still held firmly in your hands, make tiny pinches at the corners of each end.

You could also make this leaf by starting with a square and then fixing peaks to the square's edges. After that, you can then blend the edges into apices. Usually, the tweezing tool works best for crafting this leaf.

What you get should look quite similar to the one that is illustrated below;

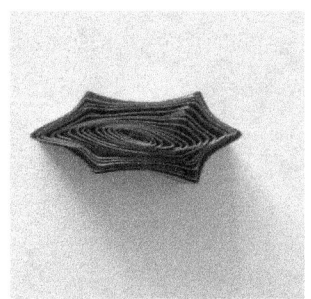

A Short message from the Author:

Hey, I hope you are enjoying the book? I would love to hear your thoughts!

Many readers do not know how hard reviews are to come by and how much they help an author.

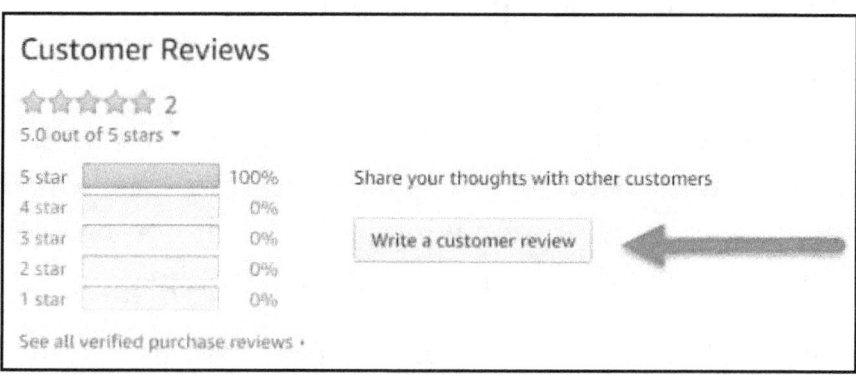

I would be incredibly grateful if you could take just 60 seconds to write a short review on Amazon, even if it is a few sentences!

>> Click here to leave a quick review

Thanks for the time taken to share your thoughts!

Chapter 4

Paper Quilling Pattern Designs

It's time to put all you have learned so far into making actual designs. So, let's get right into it.

Flower Pendant

This project focuses on the beauty of paper jewelry. Making this pendant does not require the usual technical know-how in making jewelry. All you need to know are the basic quilling techniques and tips.

Now, you'd also need to bear in mind that this pendant is not waterproof. Ensure to take it off before diving in the pool or having a shower. However, if you know you'd forget to take it off, ensure you seal it with a waterproof coating.

Tools and Supplies

- Quilling paper strips
- Glue/ Adhesive
- Slotted tool

Additional Tools and Supplies

- Jump ring
- Ready-made cord or chain
- Pearl bead (optional)
- Extra beads as embellishments for the chain (optional)

Instructions

1. Pick up the color of the paper strip you want to work with. Then, have the strip rolled into a nice coil with the aid of the slotting tool.

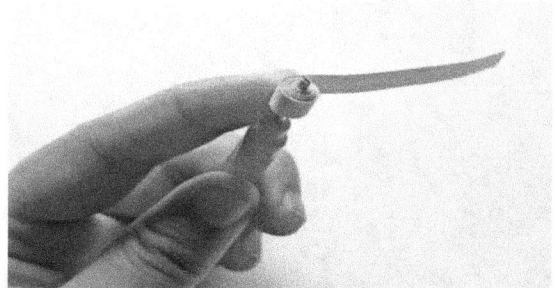

2. Once you are done rolling the strip, pull the quilling tool out of the center where it formerly lay. While bringing out the tool, you also want to ensure that you are firmly gripping the coiled strip. That way, the coils do not loosen.

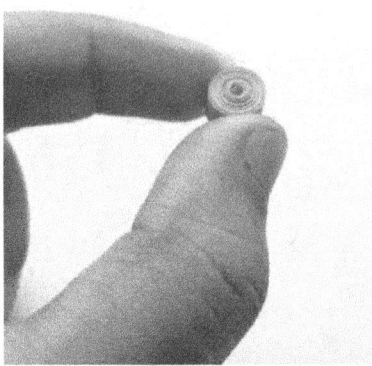

3. Reduce the pressure exerted by your fingers to allow the coils to loosen by a fraction.

4. Have the openly coiled strip sit on a regular surface before working a bead to the center with the aid of a suitable adhesive.

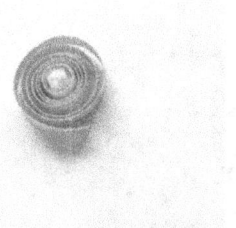

5. Have the coils tightened by gripping them with the pads of your two fingers. Then, you can proceed to have the open end pulled open. After that, you can twine the remaining strip length and fasten the tip with glue. This will be the middle of the paper quilling flower.

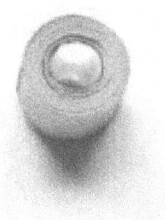

6. With a slotting tool, quill another strip. This strip should be in a different color.

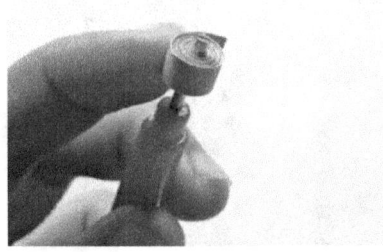

7. When you are done with the coiling, remove it from the tip of the tool.

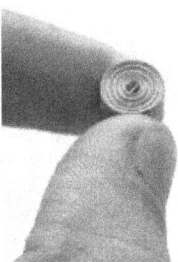

8. Leave the coil on a regular surface to loosen up a bit.

9. Pick up the open coil, and then pinch out one of the ends. This will fetch you the shape of a teardrop.

10. Pinch out the other end to have the shape of an eye.

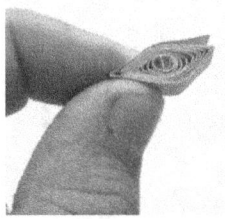

11. Go through the last five steps again to make five other eyes. The strips should be of the same color. With another color of the paper strip, make three more eyes.

12. Now, for the platform on which you'd lay all the shapes you created, you could work with a sheet of paper, plastic, or any other material. Then, fix the part that stands as the middle of the flower on

the platform. From the six eyes you have, take two and attach them to the platform as shown below while forming a circle. All you need to do is to glue any of the pointed edges to the central circle. Connect your petals by gluing the rounded parts of the eye shapes together.

13. From the other color of the coils you made, fill the middle of the circle and link the petals.

14. Continue with the technique above until you attain the proper shape of a flower.

15. Make a tight coil with a large loop at the middle.

16. Fix that coil between any two petals of the flower so that it acts as the loop. You can now apply your sealants to your project if you want to. However, you should maintain the hole you made in the coil above.

17. Connect a jump ring through the coil's loop so that your quilled flower hangs down like a pendant.

18. Next, fix the jump ring to your chain or cord. If you want to add beads, either complete the chain yourself or detach the ends that came with it and use large beads with holes as embellishments.

You are done!

Flower Frame

Flower frames are great for getting your photo albums and other pictures to look even more beautiful. It is also a very great way to get your kids busy all day long!

Tools and Supplies

- Quilling paper strips
- Glue
- Scissors
- Slotted tool
- Photo frame

Instructions

1. Two shapes were used here, the eye shape and the open (loose) coil shape

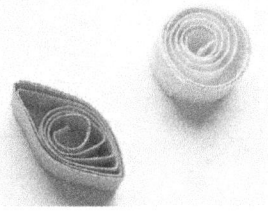

2. To make the eye shape, use a variety of colored paper strips. Create seven eye shapes for the leaves using green-colored strips, and create the loose coils with yellow-colored strips.

3. Next, attach the quilled paper strips to the surface of the frame. Begin from a corner or side. For each floral pattern, I utilized eight eye shapes; you can utilize as much as you desire. Simply use craft glue to adhere the shapes to the frame.

After you've finished making the floral pattern, glue a loose yellow coil in the center.

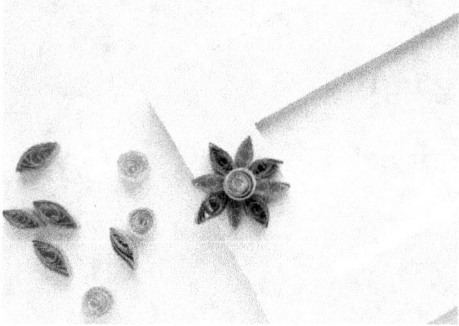

4. Continue adding quilled shapes to the frame until it is completely covered.

   First, make the floral patterns, then go on to the leaves.

5. You can make some tight coils to cover in any spaces between quilled patterns,

Let the glue dry.

You are done!

Snowflake

Snowflakes are reminders of the chilly seasons and are very spectacular to observe. You can get them from the falling snow, and yes, when you pick them up, you'd never get two that match up in all dimensions. We would be making some of these pretty snowflakes in a bit. The only difference would be that ours won't be cold!

Tools and Supplies

- Quilling paper strips of various colors
- Slotted tool
- Scissors
- Craft glue

Instructions

1. For each snowflake, choose two different colors. Make twelve 12-inch-long quilling strips (6 of each hue) and thirteen 6-inch-long quilling strips (seven of the first color and six of the second).

2. Using the slotted quilling tool, coil one of the 12 inch long strips completely. Remove the coil from the tool and loosen it up a tad bit.

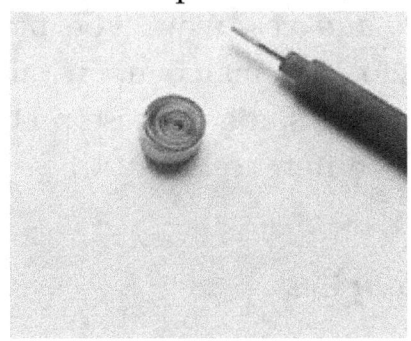

3. Make a teardrop pattern by pressing any side of the loose coil. Now press the side that was previously squeezed on the opposite side. This will result in the creation of a lens shape or what you know as the eye shape.

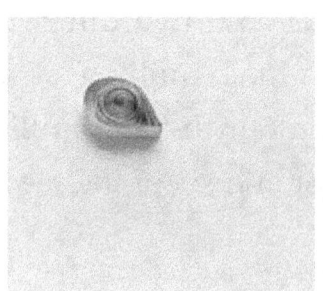 

4. Use the same strips of color to make five more eyes shapes, giving you six eye shapes on the whole.

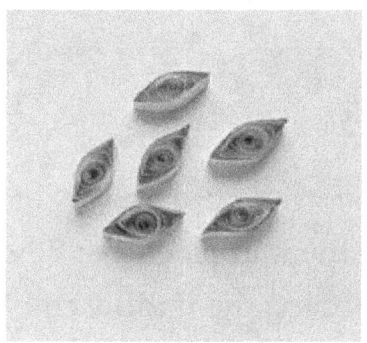

5. Make 6 teardrop shapes with the second color of 12-inch quilling strips.

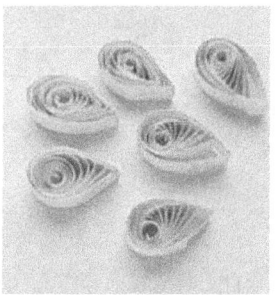

6. Use the 6" quilling strips of the first color to make 7 loose coils. Make 6 extra loose coils with the second color's 6" quilling strips.

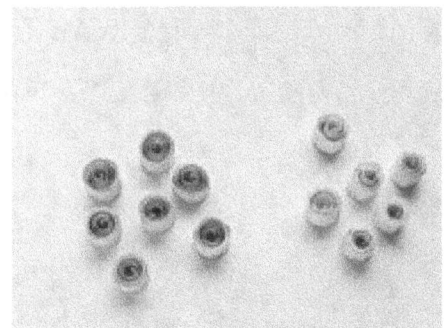

7. Take the color-coordinated set of seven loose coils. Glue them in place in a flower pattern with 6 coils encircling the middle coil.

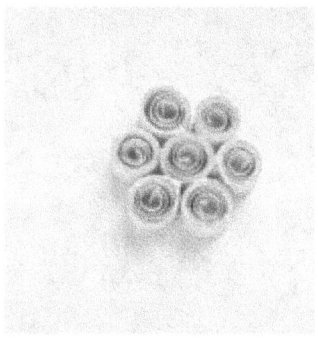

8. Glue each quilled eye shape between the open (loose) coils in the flower you just made.

9. Glue the teardrop shapes between the eye shapes, with the sharp side facing outward and the curved side bonded with loose coils with glue.

10. Finally, glue the last six open coils to the tip of the eye or teardrop shapes

11. Repeat with different colors of snowflakes and allow the glue to dry fully.

You are done! You could stick the quilled paper flakes to some Christmas card, Christmas tree or even adorn your room by suspending them from the ceiling via cords.

Necklace and Earring

If you cherish jewelry and other ornaments, then you should work on this project.

Tools and Supplies

- Paper strips of dimension 4mm. You should get about five different colors.
- Slotted tool
- Glue
- Scissors

Additional Tools

- Jewelry pliers
- Jump rings (about 10mm)
- Necklace
- Hooks for earrings

Instructions

Quilled Earrings

1. In your first color, create a tight coil out of a whole strip of quilling paper, then extra three out

of 10cm strips and glue them together. In your second color, create three teardrops out of 15cm strips, then glue them in place.

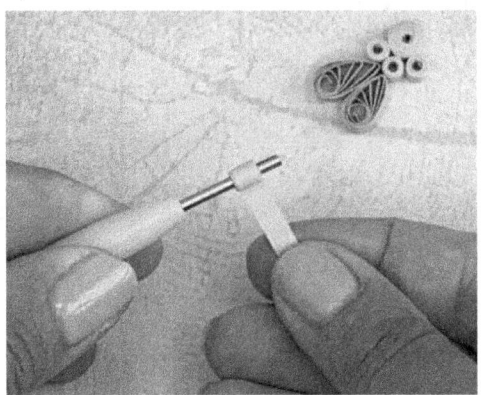

2. In your third color, create three tight coils out of an entire strip and glue them under the teardrops. In your fourth color, create extra three teardrops out of 20cm strips, then glue them in place under the tight coils.

3. In your fifth color, create three tight coils out of complete strips and glue them under the teardrops. From a 10cm strip of the same color, roll a tight coil, then glue to the bottom.

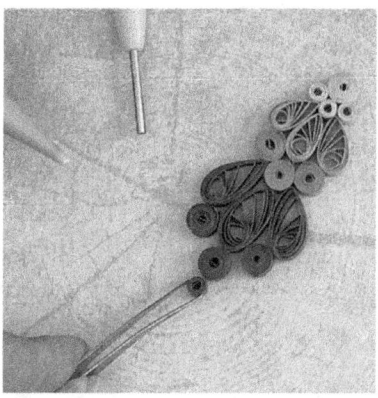

4. In your fifth color, create two 10cm tight coils, then glue them at the bottom in between the tight

coils. Create two more in your third color, then glue them together on either side of the tight coils. To the top, add a jump ring and hook for the earring.

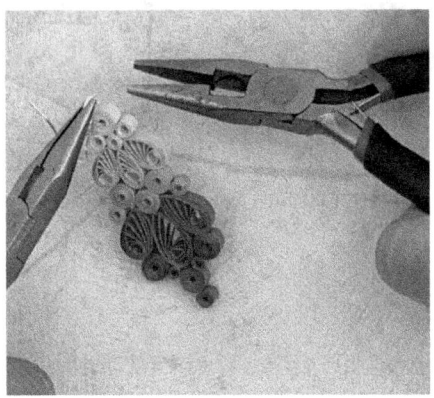

Quilled Necklace

1. In your first color, create three tight rolls out of complete quilling paper strips, then six out of 10cm strips. Create two teardrops out of 15cm strips of the same color and glue them together as illustrated.

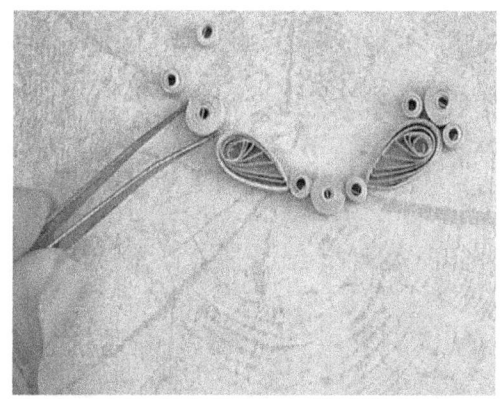

2. In your second color's complete strips, create three teardrops and two from 15cm strips, then glue them in place. Create four tight coils out of complete strips of your third color and two out of 15cm strips, gluing in between them.

3. In your fourth color, create three half-moons (as shown below) out of complete strips and glue them under the teardrops.

4. In your fifth color, create three tight coils out of complete strips, then glue them underneath the half-moons. Create a tight coil out of a 20cm strip and three 6cm strips in the same color, then glue them together beneath.

5. Add jump rings to the top of the tight coils, then use jewelry pliers to cut a chain necklace in half, attaching the jump rings to the ends.

   You are done!

Butterfly

Butterflies have so many beautiful wings and bodies. We will be working with several colors for this project while blending them. This project is a bit more complex than the earlier projects, so brace up for a bit of a twist.

Tools and Supplies

- Strips of quilling paper (black, red, dark orange, light orange, and yellow)
- Glue/ Adhesive
- Scissors
- Slotted tool
- Quilling template board

Additional Tools and Supplies

- Styrofoam for pinning the shapes
- A Monarch butterfly template. You could get one from the internet.

Instructions

1. Make coils by joining paper strips

Several of these coils (circles) are made up of multiple hues. To begin, tear (not cut) your strips to the proper length. This will result in a smoother connection. Then use adhesive to fuse them together.

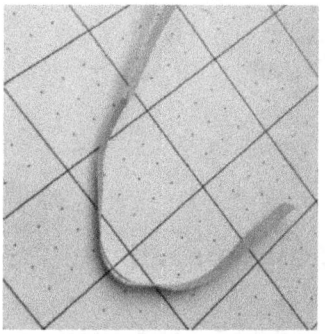

Once the glue is dry, roll up the strips and use a slotted quilling tool to produce loose coils (circles). Insert the coils in the template board and let the template loose. If necessary, adjust the coils. Glue the ends together with care.

I've listed the sizes of the strips and coils to be created in the next stage. There are also some simple shapes to make.

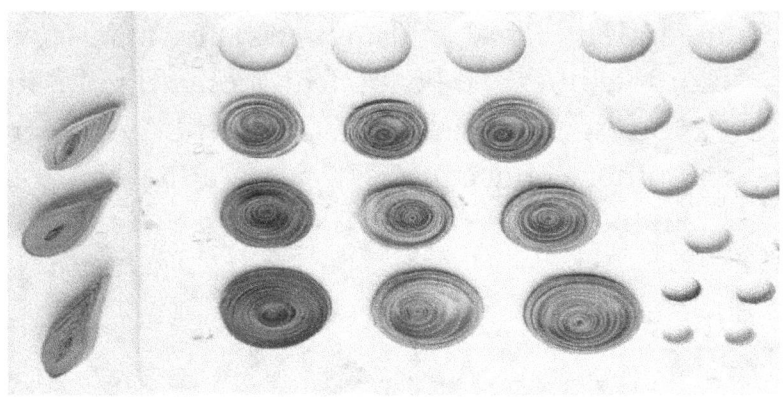

2. Prepare the coils and shapes

I've attempted to make this as simple as possible to recreate. The length of the strip, as well as the color and circle size, are captured in the diagram below. I've chosen the initials to help you remember the colors because they're so similar.

All of the tight yellow coils (circles) were rolled in 4-inch strips of paper

2.5-inch paper strips were used to roll all of the tight white coils (circles)

I used a variety of lengths for the rest. I've taken shorter lengths for some larger coils (circles) in the past because it allowed me to build thin but lengthy shapes.

Create loose coils per the coil (circle) sizes specified in the diagram below, then compress them to shape as shown below.

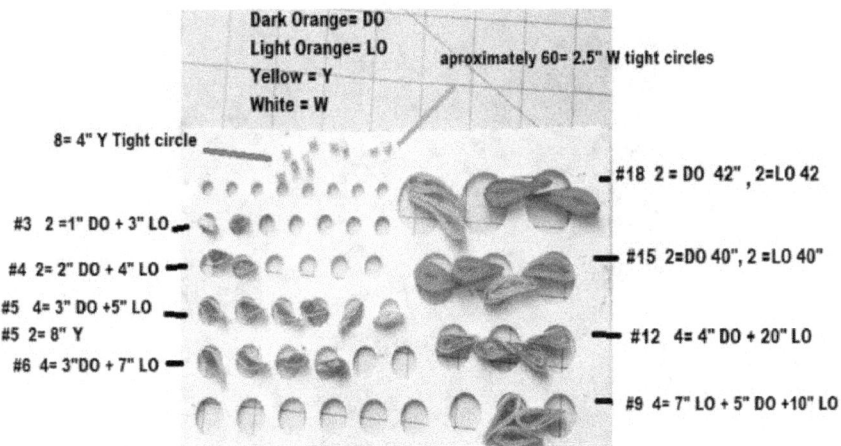

3. Make a teardrop shape by pressing one end of the loose or open coil (circle)

4. Make the shape of a leaf

   To make the Leaf shape, squeeze the ends of a loose coil. You can twist the shape in whichever direction you choose if you want it to be more curled.

   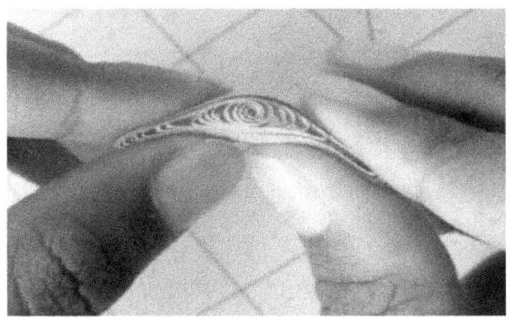

5. Use black to wrap

   The white dots were rolled separately. However, when working on this technique, I discovered that I should have joined a black strip to the white and rolled everything at a go to create the white tight coils needed for the outline.

   Though this is fine for most white dot shapes, for others, you'll have to bridge the gaps with white tights coils and black loose coils. You'll see what I'm implying when you take a look at the stages below.

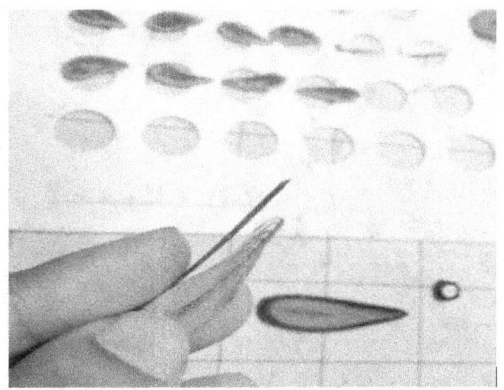

Glue the black strip to the other shapes and outline them. Ensure to bend the black strip further from the one you last bent while wrapping it up to resemble the traditional paper quilling shape. It would also be thinner at the end, making it easier to blend it into the shape. This was done while I was putting the pieces together to make the black thick or thin as needed.

The coiled-up quilled strips may try to come out in the larger coils. Simply put glue between the strips to remedy the problem.

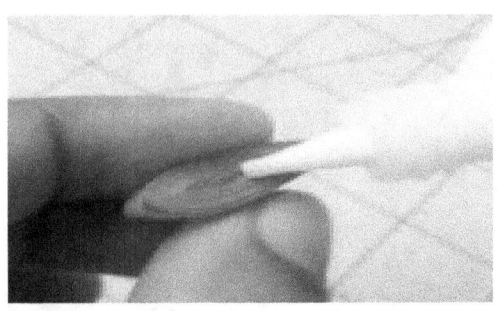

6. Make the upper wings

Assemble the butterfly using the Monarch butterfly image you got off the internet as guidance. I assembled on a Styrofoam platform, so it was simple pinning the shapes in place.

Because this is primarily a visual instruction, it is difficult to explain all of the procedures in writing because you would not comprehend them. As a result, I've labeled the parts and sizes in the images. Ensure to work in pairs as well because it would be easier to make the wings symmetrical this way.

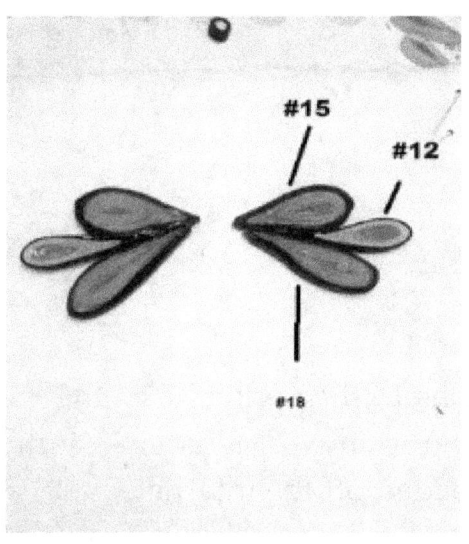

After completing the main body, I placed the yellow and white tight coils in their correct positions. I wrapped these coils in black depending on how much space I wanted to fill. I wanted a large black region to fill when putting this wing together. So I created circle #18 by gluing a white tight coil to an 18-inch black long strip.

I sketched the wing on the Styrofoam by following my Monarch butterfly image downloaded off the internet.

After gluing a strip of black paper to the butterfly's edge, I gradually took the shape with the strip in filling the gaps with the black and white quilled coils. A few of the black coils are bigger or formed in a teardrop or leaf shape to fill in the gap.

After you've finished filling in the gaps, go over the entire shape using a black paper strip to serve as an outline. Repeat the process two times.

7. Make the lower wings

As with the upper wings, use your butterfly image as a guide to position the wings. You can go on to the white dots once you've finished making the basic shape with the petals.

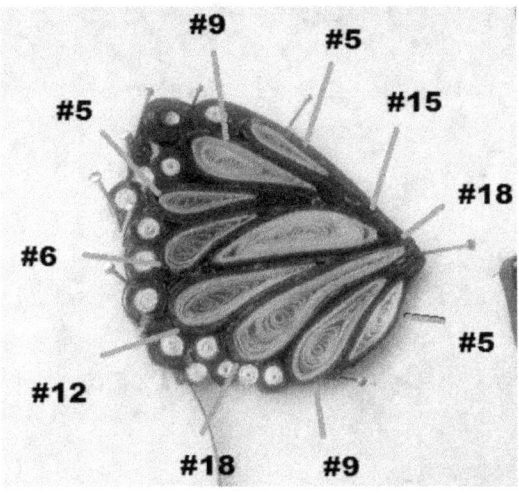

You may not always be able to proceed exactly as shown in the image, but attempt to get a closer version of it as possible. Go over the shape with a black long strip roughly twice as you did with the preceding wings. It should be glued down.

8. Make the body

   Put half of your wings together as the wings of a butterfly are. Now take a measurement to discover how long it will take you to make your body.

   I made a 1.5-inch wide by 3-inch long triangle for my body. Begin rolling from the wide side. Ensure that the point is always in the middle. Before you finish rolling, dab a little glue on it and stick it down.

   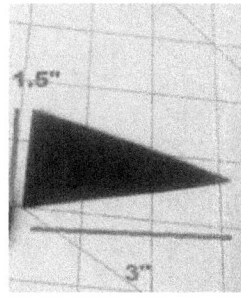 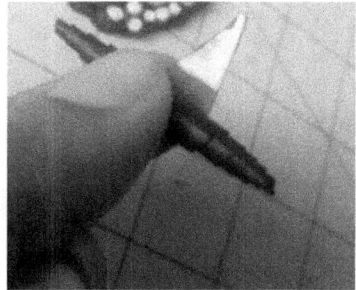

For the head, repeat the procedures but use a triangle that is 0.25-inch wide and 3-inch long. Attach the head to the body using glue.

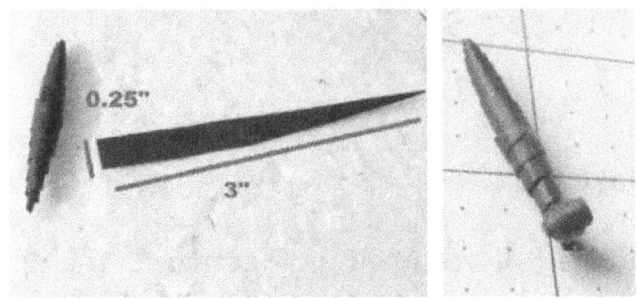

Cut a 3-inch long piece of 1mm strip. To make a 'V' shape, fold it in half. Roll the end half-way down and secure it with glue. Attach the antlers to the head using glue.

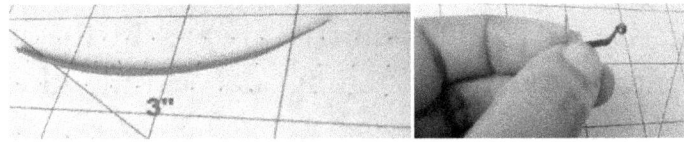

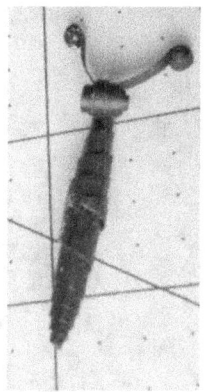

9. Assemble the butterfly parts

   To assemble, arrange your wings on the body as desired. Use objects to push up the body so that the wings may be glued at an angle.

   This takes a long time because you need it to dry thoroughly before gluing the lower wings. You could also use hot glue.

You are done!

Birthday Cake

This project can serve as an embellishment for your home during birthday ceremonies and other exciting events. You can also use it to decorate your child's Barbie playhouse.

Tools and Supplies

- Slotted tool
- Glue
- Scissors
- Quilling paper strips;
    - 10mm of 18 or 20 strips of lavender color.
    - 10mm of 10 strips of pink color
    - 10mm of 3 or 4 strips of white color

5mm of 3 shiny-red strips

- 3mm of 1 yellow-orange strip

Note: The bigger the cake size, the more the strips you'd need.

Instructions

1. Make the cake layers

   Use glue to adhere the lavender-colored 10 mm paper strip to the top of another lavender-colored strip. Continue in this manner until all of the lavender-colored strips are connected.

   Make a big coil by quilling this long strip with a slotted quilling tool.

   Make a coil out of the white-colored strips the same way as before; however, it should be smaller than the last one.

   Duplicate with pink strips; however, the coil should be smaller than the white coil this time. Make sure all of the coils are secure). The cake's three layers are now ready.

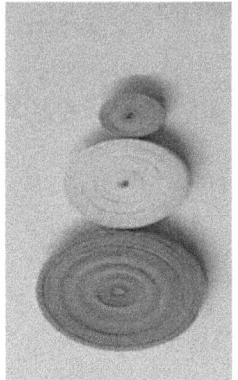

2. Make the parts for the ribbons, bow, and candle

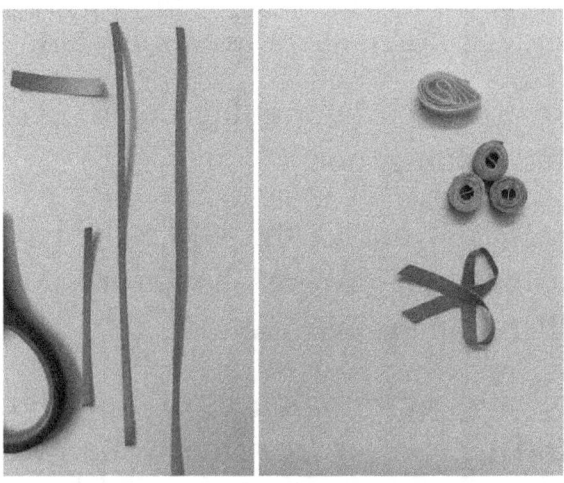

Now, as seen in the figure, cut two to three 5mm shiny red-colored strips from the middle. These will be the ribbons for the layers of our Birthday Cake.

These strips can also be used to make a bow for decoration and to make the candle, as seen in the image.

Take and coil (loose coil) 1/4 of the yellow-orange strip. Then, form a teardrop shape out of this coil. This will be the candle's flame.

3. Decorate the cake

Place the ribbons in the middle of each cake layer and glue them in place.

Now use glue to fuse the little coils together to form the candle's body and add the teardrop shape to the top and glue.

4. Assemble the cake

   Place the layers one on top of the other in the following order:

   Big coil (bottom) - Medium coil (Center) - Small coil (top)

Place the candle on top of the cake's top layer and put the bow on it as well.

Your cake is ready!

You may also make cakes in a variety of colors and sizes.

Birthday Card

Sometimes, handmade birthday cards are more beautiful and appreciated than their printed counterpart. That is why this project will revolve around learning the intricacies of making this type of quilled craft. It's simple, easy, and beginner-friendly!

Tools and Supplies

- Slotted tool
- Glue
- Scissors
- Quilling paper strips

Additional Tools and Supplies

- White card
- Circles of colored paper
- Stamps (optional)

Instructions

1. You'd start by making three triangles from the quilling paper.

    To make the triangles, all you need is to pick up your quilling paper (orange-colored paper was used here). Twist the paper into a coil with the aid of a slotted quilling tool.

After that, let the coil loosen up a bit.

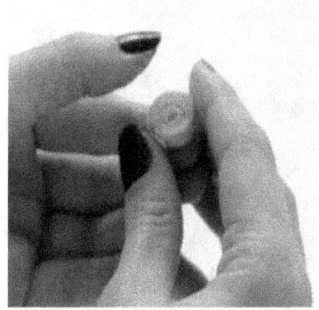

Pinch the edges out at precise points. This should give you a triangle. You should repeat this procedure two more times to get about three triangles.

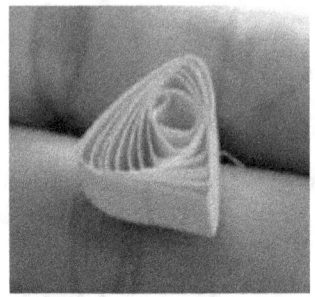

2. Make 6 teardrop shapes using different colors of paper strips
3. Make a rectangular shape using a green paper strip, then use orange and yellow strips to make the flame.

Apply glue on the birthday card and fix the shapes on the card.

4. Next, run glue across one side of a purple-colored strip, then fix it to the front of the card.

You can also fix the purple strip to the back too. This step is not compulsory, though. You could do without the purple strips altogether, but it gives your card some little glamor.

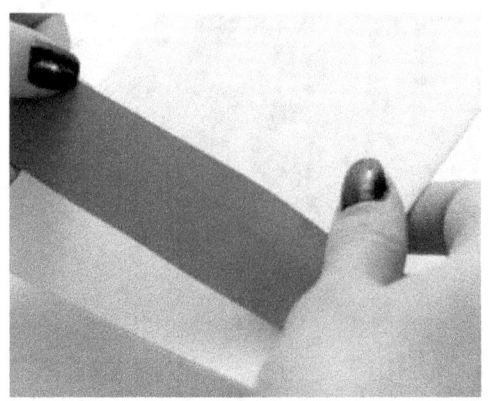

5. Fix the circles to the surface of the card. You could work with templates or punching tools to make circular paper strips. After forming the circles, affix them to the surface of the card.

6. Add whatever notes you wish inside the card. This is where the stamps work best. Using stamps is optional.

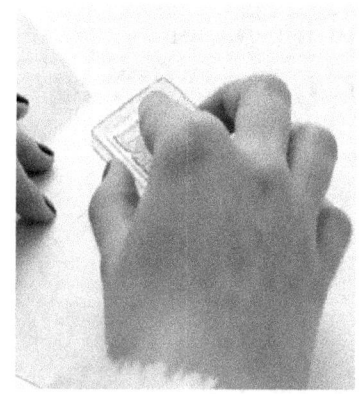

You are done!

Owl

This is another project that you can do as a hobby. It is quite easy to make and is great for both adults and kids.

Tools and Supplies

- Strips of quilling paper
- Slotted tool
- Scissors
- Glue
- Colored craft paper

Instructions

1. Choose a color with which you'd begin the coils. Then, with a strip of quilling paper that measures about 12 inches, make a coil with your slotting tool. The coils should be wound tightly around the mouth or tip of the tool.

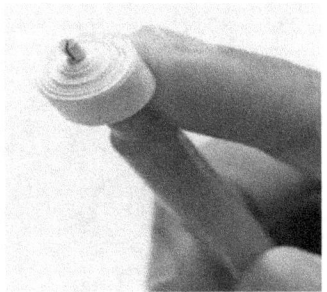

2. With another strip of quilling paper that measures about 12 inches, make another coil, and then ensure that the open end stays at the

outermost edges. The coils of this new color should go around that of the former coils. Ensure that the coils are still gripped tightly around the mouth of the tool. Fix a thin layer of glue at the end of the coil to hold it in place.

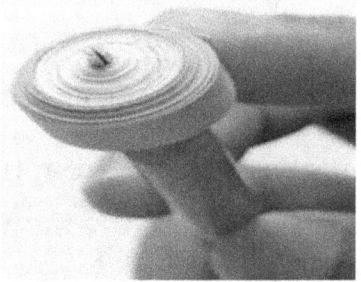

3. When you are done with the coils above, remove them from the mouth of the tool and then, allow it to free up a bit.

4. To get a shape that looks like a teardrop, apply minimal pressure to one edge of the open coil.

5. Leave a gap of about 2cm from the first point you pressed. Then, apply a little more pressure to one of the sides so that you get the shape of a teardrop again. That shape will end up being formed is a bunny's ear which will become the body of the owl.

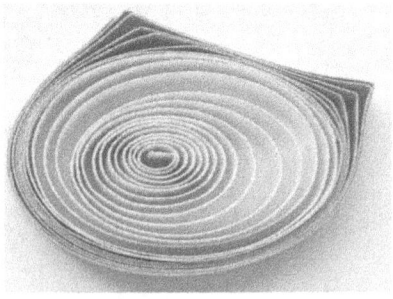

6. With a quilling strip that measures about 20" in length, make another bunny ear. The shape you get from here should be in a dimension that is smaller than the first one. This will stand for the head of the owl. To make the wings, you'd make two marquise (eye) shapes from an 8" long strip (we discussed this in the **paper quilling basic shapes** section). Also, make two **curved** marquise shapes for the eyebrows of the owl using the same strip. Also, use two 6" strips to make two triangles (legs) and a 6" strip to make a square shape for the beak.

When making the eyes, work with a black strip of about 12" length. Twist the strip so that you get a closed coil. After that, make another closed coil of about 10" length with another color of the paper strip around the first coil. Then repeat this coil

7. Smear a thin layer of glue to a colored craft paper, outlining the whole shape of the owl—the body and the head of the owl.

8. Fix the quilled body and the head to the craft paper.

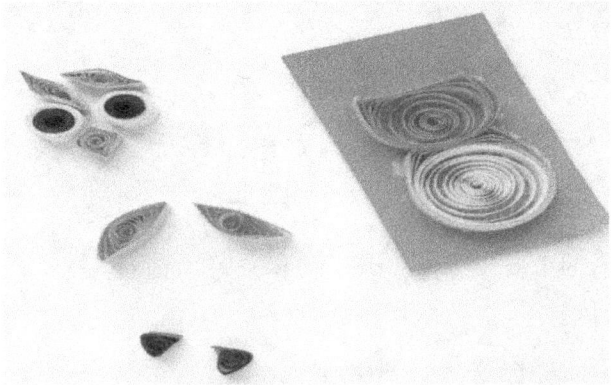

9. Attach the eyes and the beak to the head.

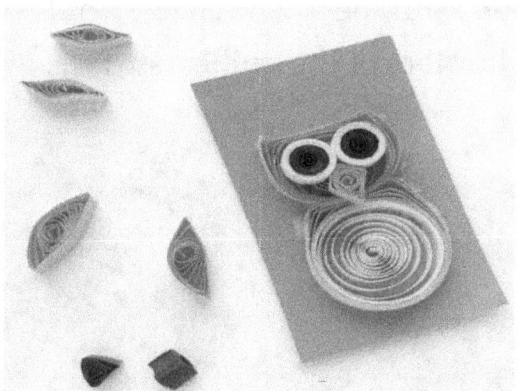

10. Fix the curved marquise shapes to the areas above the eyes. Then, leave the glue to dry

11. With a pair of scissors, cut around the head and the body of the owl. Then, gently cut out the outer borders of the quilled surface.

12. Fix the quilled legs and the wings (the first quilled marquise shape) to the major body. This step will finish the quilled owl.

Leave the glue to dry, and you are done!

Chapter 5

Fixing Paper Quilling Common Mistakes

You could make tons of mistakes as a beginner in this craft, which is okay. However, before you go all hard on yourself, most of these mistakes aren't that bad and can be resolved and/ or avoided altogether.

Lets's take a look at some of these common mistakes.

1. **The issue of excess glue:** This issue is by far the most commonest mistake that beginners make. Your whole quilling project can turn out to be a great mess when you use lots of glue. However, this issue can be avoided. Because of how light paper is, it is doesn't need much glue. So, you need something that can help you regulate the rate you apply glue to your quilling project.

   Earlier in this book, we talked about a bottle with a specialized mouth. These bottles have heads that are highly capable of restricting the total volume of glue that runs out through the mouth the moment you apply considerable pressure to its sides.

Now, what happens when you have already made the mistake of applying excess glue? You'd notice that the excess glue would bleed at the sides as the paper strip presses down on it. This excess glue can be removed by running the edges of a flat card across the surface in a very swift and neat way.

2. **Chunks of dry glue**: The area where you'd find a lot of these chunks are your fingers. You know, every time you try to ensure that the glue doesn't come out to be too much, a little or even most of it jumps right to your fingers and glues itself there. You might not feel the effect at first, but then, as the layers begin to rise, you begin to feel pretty uncomfortable.

That is why it is more than necessary that you have a damp rag beside you. With that, you can clean up the pads and lengths of your fingers as you progress with your project.

Also, when you find the chunks forming a frame around the coiled strips, you could work with tools with sharp edges. These sharp edges would help to remove the chunks. An example of such tools are needles.

3. **Asymmetrical coils:** This issue is another very common mistake that beginners make. The solution to this issue comes out to be very easy actually. All you need to do is ensure that you use your two hands while crafting. One hand should do the centralization, and the other should do the edging. That way, you can control where the middle of the coil sits.

Another way by which you can avoid this issue is by working with quilling template boards. These boards were discussed in the pages of this book. They help prevent the coils from getting too loose while being made.

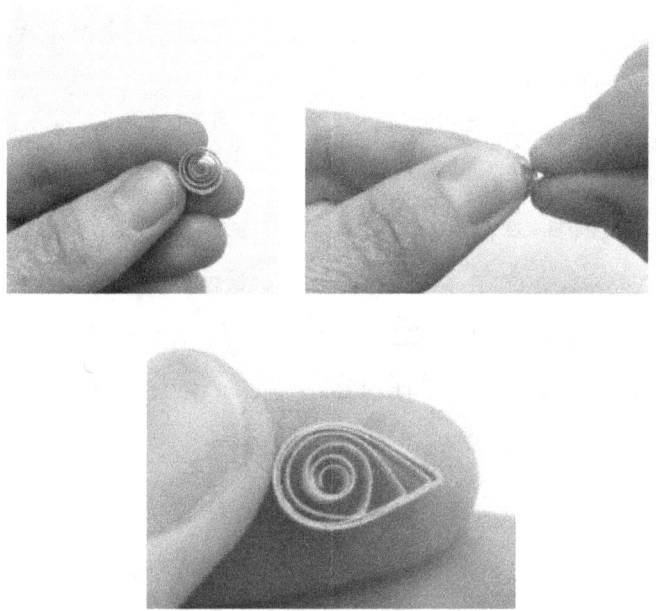

4. **Rough background:** The background of your quilling project becomes wrinkled because the paper used is too thin to support the glue used to attach your work.

When mounting my quillings, I prefer to use a thick mat board. It's quite powerful! Another idea is only to use a small amount of adhesive. Instead of coating the entire item before mounting, use tiny dots. If you want a more attractive background, use spray adhesive or matte Mod

Podge to adhere to patterned scrapbook paper to mat board.

The possibilities for color and pattern are infinite!

5. **Uneven drying of quilled shapes**: As your pieces dry on your workboard, it might be difficult to ensure they are all completely level. You may not realize a section has come off until it's too late!

This is a scenario that I find myself in frequently, and the quick fix is to use a craft knife. I glide the blade between the two shapes causing me problems lightly (very carefully!). They come apart, and all I have to do now is reassemble them with glue.

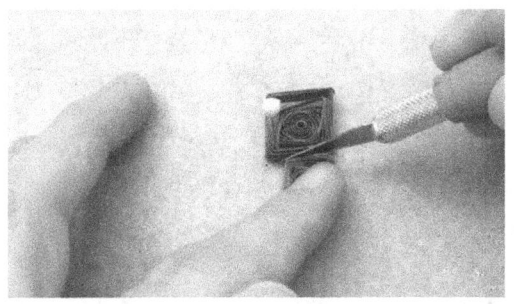

However, I would not advocate this option to the faint of heart. There's a considerable probability the coils will be damaged or deformed by accident. The simplest way to avoid this issue is to examine for evenness with a finger or a sharp tool before the pieces dry.

6. **The presence of air bubbles around thick double strips:** I like to produce double-thick quilling strips for edge work. While putting consistent glue all the way through is the most critical stage in constructing these strips, there will be occasions when there is a gap. And that gap in the glue will cause your strip to bubble. It's usually something you don't notice until you're working on a project with the strip. And you're not going to want to take the whole thing out by then, are you? I've discovered that snipping the

bubble with those tiny scissors is a terrific option. Apply a small amount of glue to the remaining ends and hold in place with tweezers or a pin until it dries.

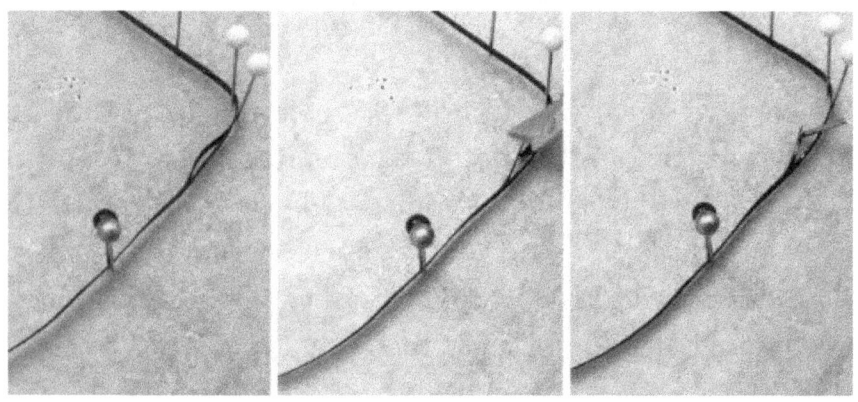

There you go, good as new!

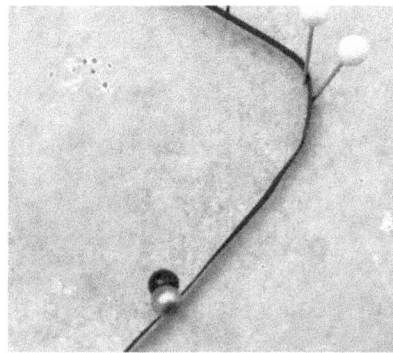

The end... almost!

Hey! We've made it to the final chapter of this book, and I hope you've enjoyed it so far.

If you have not done so yet, I would be incredibly thankful if you could take just a minute to leave a quick review on Amazon

Reviews are not easy to come by, and as an independent author with a little marketing budget, I rely on you, my readers, to leave a short review on Amazon.

Even if it is just a sentence or two!

So if you really enjoyed this book, please...

\>\> Click here to leave a brief review on Amazon.

I truly appreciate your effort to leave your review, as it truly makes a huge difference.

Chapter 6

Paper Quilling FAQs

To wrap up our paper quilling journey, we will discuss peculiar questions that quillers typically ask when working on their quilling projects. While going through this section, please pay attention to every detail, as it can help prevent you from making the same mistakes they made.

1. **What kind of quilling paper should I work with as a beginner?**

    First, you need to know that the best strips of paper that you'd want to use to practice your quilling should be about 3mm in length. You could also make a couple of requests online as you go further into the craft. Paper brands like the Quilled Creations in the United States of America are good suppliers of quilling paper; this does not mean you can't get great quilling papers on Amazon and the likes. Paper is not costly, so you'd find out that you can easily get the strips in any color or size.

2. How long does it take to be a pro at this craft?

All you need for this craft might be a couple of strips of paper, glue, and some other tools. But then, yes, this craft still has a whole lot of technicalities attached to it. Depending on how seriously you take the craft, you will find these supposed technicalities difficult or easy. It also depends on how willing you are to learn something new. With the right amount of willingness and creativity, you would surely be good to go and become a pro in no time!

3. Which quilling paper will fetch me the best coils?

There are different kinds of quilling paper out there: plain colors, pearl-stained ones, metallic paper sheets, and patterned ones. Each of these paper categories can give you different and peculiar results. However, note that the paper used for quilling is thicker and softer than the regular paper. Also, most of the quilling sheets you would find in stores, for example, have been organized into different colors and dimensions.

4. What tools do you recommend I use?

The slotting tool is a very great tool for quilling your projects. Some dislike that it leaves crimps to the base of their project, so they seek alternatives. However, you can solve this issue by getting a slotting tool that will only cause insignificant crimping. You could also work with needles when you do not want the crimp at the base of your project or anywhere.

5. What is the most appropriate glue that I can use for my project?

If you are going to buy a bottle of glue, you want to ensure that it is clear and relatively dense. The transparent gels are the best kinds of glue you want to work with. They have no bad smell and also will not smear your coils with unnecessary stains. You also want to get glue with a special mouth that can regulate the rate at which you apply the glue to your project.

6. What exactly are the dimensions that my open coils should have?

There's no particular requirement for your open coils. All you need to bear in mind is how you have your paper strip wound up. To get a uniform coil dimension, you might want to work with a circular sizing tool. You should also ensure that you roll the coils tightly against each other.

7. How can you deal with cramping fingers?

Know that cramps occur when you grip your tool too hard. It could also occur when you continue to work without stopping for once. It would help if you allowed your fingers to rest for some time before getting back to work. If the grip area of your tools is too uncomfortable, you can wound a nice tape around its span.

8. How can quilling paper be preserved?

The best place to preserve the strips of your quilling paper is in a dry, dust-free place. Keeping the paper where the sun's rays won't get to will also do a great job of preserving the paper. Remember, paper is made from pulp, making it very susceptible to fading. That is more reason you should protect the pieces from the sun.

Conclusion

Paper quilling is super easy, yet it is an intricate craft that requires you to put in a lot of creativity, hard work, and meticulousness. Quilled crafts are mostly adorned with charming embellishment, resulting in a stunning paper quilled masterpiece. Paper quilling can be used to make a variety of designs, such as jewelry, frames, cards, animals, and more. This craft can be enjoyed by both children and adults, who can create delightful paper quilling masterpieces for both friends and family. The supplies required for these designs are mostly inexpensive, which is a fantastic motivator for new quillers.

With every tip and knowledge shared in the pages of this book, you should now be well informed on virtually everything there is to know in the art of paper quilling, which should spur you into infusing your ingenuity in making eye-catchy paper quilling pieces of art.

Quillers, have fun quilling!

www.ingramcontent.com/pod-product-compliance
Lightning Source LLC
Chambersburg PA
CBHW071419070526
44578CB00003B/617